Lexile: _____70L_____

AR/BL: _____2.3_____

AR Points: _____0.5_____

Pebble®

My Family

Foster Families

by Sarah L. Schuette

Consulting Editor: Gail Saunders-Smith, PhD

CAPSTONE PRESS
a capstone imprint

Pebble Books are published by Capstone Press,
151 Good Counsel Drive, P.O. Box 669, Mankato, Minnesota 56002.
www.capstonepress.com

092009
005618CGS10

Books published by Capstone Press are manufactured with paper
containing at least 10 percent post-consumer waste.

Library of Congress Cataloging-in-Publication Data
Schuette, Sarah L., 1976–
    Foster families / by Sarah L. Schuette.
    p. cm. — (Pebble books. My family)
    Includes bibliographical references and index.
    Summary: "Simple text and photographs present foster families, including
how family members interact with one another" — Provided by publisher.
    ISBN 978-1-4296-3979-8 (library binding)
    ISBN 978-1-4296-4837-0 (paperback)
    1. Foster children — Juvenile literature. 2. Foster parents — Juvenile literature.
I. Title. II. Series.
HQ759.7.S35 2010
306.874 — dc22   2009023388

Note to Parents and Teachers

The My Family set supports national social studies standards
related to identifying family members and their roles in the family.
This book describes and illustrates foster families. The images
support early readers in understanding the text. The repetition of
words and phrases helps early readers learn new words. This book
also introduces early readers to subject-specific vocabulary words,
which are defined in the Glossary section. Early readers may need
assistance to read some words and to use the Table of Contents,
Glossary, Read More, Internet Sites, and Index sections of the book.

Table of Contents

4

About Foster Families

Foster families
take care of children
whose parents cannot.

foster father

foster mother

foster daughter

foster daughter

5

Foster children sometimes
return to live
with their parents.

Some foster families adopt their foster children. Other children are adopted by new families.

Helping

Foster family members
help each other.
Jayla and her foster parents
paint her bedroom.

Erin's foster mother helps her make a scrapbook.

Kelly's foster grandmother teaches her how to knit.

Having Fun

Foster family members have fun together. Linda and her foster sister play dress up.

Noah and his foster brother play a game of horseshoes.

Foster family members love each other.

Glossary

adopt — to make a child a legal member of a family

horseshoes — a game in which a U-shaped piece of metal is thrown around a metal stake

knit — to loop yarn together to make clothing or other projects

member — a part of a group or family

parent — a mother or a father

scrapbook — a memory book filled with art projects, pictures, and written notes

Read More

Clark, Jan. *Family Survival.* Kids' Guides. Chicago: Raintree, 2005.

Levete, Sarah. *Fostering and Adoption.* Let's Talk About. North Mankato, Minn.: Stargazer Books, 2007.

Nelson, Julie. *Kids Need to Be Safe: A Book for Young Children in Foster Care.* Kids Are Important. Minneapolis: Free Spirit, 2006.

Internet Sites

FactHound offers a safe, fun way to find Internet sites related to this book. All of the sites on FactHound have been researched by our staff.

Here's all you do:

Visit *www.facthound.com*

FactHound will fetch the best sites for you!

23

Index

Word Count: 92
Grade: 1
Early-Intervention Level: 10

Editorial Credits
Gillia Olson, editor; Juliette Peters, designer; Sarah Schuette, photo stylist;
    Marcy Morin, studio scheduler; Eric Manske, production specialist

Photo Credits
All photos by Capstone Studio/Karon Dubke

The Capstone Press Photo Studio thanks Countryside Homes, in Mankato, Minn.,
for its help with photo shoots for this book.

The author dedicates this book in memory of her friend Marion Moenke, who
was like a foster grandmother.